I Didn't Know Kyoto

poems by

Sheppard Ranbom

Finishing Line Press
Georgetown, Kentucky

I Didn't Know Kyoto

Publisher: Leah Huete de Maines
Editor: Christen Kincaid
Cover Art: Ginkgo fallen leaves and couple, by 綾花 木下 Ayaka Kinoshite,
        Adobe Stock Images ID 318219771
Author Photo: Johanne Hjort
Cover Design: Michael Molanphy

Order online: www.finishinglinepress.com
        also available on amazon.com

Author inquiries and mail orders:
Finishing Line Press
PO Box 1626
Georgetown, Kentucky 40324
USA

Table of Contents

Even in Kyoto
hearing the cry of the cuckoo
I long for Kyoto.
—*Bashō* (translated by Robert Haas)

Pearl

Desire does not fade:
its faults cure with age.
I drown in the liquor
of her breath, a keepsake
held in nacreous layers
of memory, a secret
still-hooded pearl.

Caesar's Palace

I read Catullus by the pool.
The palace shines with dripping
flesh on *chaises longues* of gold
and silver. Highballs glisten
on tables. The sun is a heat lamp,
bright as the lemon slice in my glass.
Each street is Shibuya, and every woman
looks like someone I left 30 years ago.
Writing in piped-in oxygen,
my output amounts to
the residue soot on a lamp.

Zig zag

She showed me once
how she learned (in school)
to evade alligators.

O sad lumberer—
why must you be drawn
to that blue dress

that moves like water,
this way and that, inviting,
spoiling each advance?

Brushstroke

The masseuse scales my back
to walk the vertebrae path–
weightless parasol
of a butterfly's wings.

Gift

A cup of nectar on the stair
the orange-winged monarch returns
to lite on my tongue
answering no summons
but temptation.

Groom

(after Yosano Akiko)

Combing my unkempt hair,
she moves breathless around me,
lithe as the scarf of sunlight
she places on my shoulders.
Her turn to be groomed,
she guides my brush till
her own hair is tangled.

Afterglow

The fireflies gather in my stare—
each wink an unfilled promise,
a mark of want hovering in midair.

Barn swallows

(In memory of George C. Hudson)

I hold the *sensei's* feet as he stretches
his long torso to set the roofing tiles.
I am clumsy with the hammer
and have a fear of heights
but am at home at this angle
as he shows me how to see
upside-down, spit the nail in place,
and hold the illusion by the bootstrap.
It is not the nail that grips,
the stitching of the steel pins
in their hidden pattern,
but the sound of barn swallows
in the breath of night
that holds me still.

Asura

In the main hall of the Kofukuji
Asura's hands and faces,
three-by-three, capture
every human mood.

This face: the most beautiful.
The unsettling settles to smile
through burning tears.

Japon

*(on reading Takamura Kōtarō's "Comic Verse Given
to European Poets who Amuse Themselves with the Orient")*

The chronicler of the unnatural
calls this pure slosh—*Japon, Japon....*
saying: "You are the crazed
mother who thirsts
for your son's bloom,
a wine-mad Maenad,
unhinged and dangerous,
making us question
the sanity of praise
when you try to wear us
like a tall blonde wig
to feel beautiful again."

Takuboku

Self-important wastrel—
you'd spend your child's milk money
on your next romp,
but your words
sounded from
your frozen straits
pierce the rock of judgment
and this heart of bone
like the Hakodate wind.

Tanizaki

Such generosity to let us lick (with you)
a well-turned heel, or infantilize
a stepmother's breast, or tongue
a Dad's mistress' savory lunchbox,
peckish for her reticent love.

I am your royal retainer,
standing under the drip line of your shite,
with your swordsman's lust
to castrate a rival's face or catch
a court lady's defecation.

Let us seek perverse beauty
in glandular imagination,
and in every modern guise,
to hail our inevitable downfall,
the teasing immanence of waste.

Wedding poem

Making out with an old friend
who pulled me into a cloak room
before her second wedding,
the wine of ceremony
is poison to us now.

My role is to read
my poem about
the lonely man's escape
from himself:

For some find liberation
giving up the promiscuous
dream to be grafted to another,
finding in a small flat
looking out the double-
paned window
more room to grow…

I leave the dais to sit quietly
with the one who has become
part of my own skin,
who lives the words
and vows I can only write.

Pivot

Proper as the judge's wife who strode
Route 5 naked under her fur stole,
you enter my bedroom study
dressed in the vestment of a hand towel,
posed for applause for your splendor
and for each wisp of unpinned hair,
as you pivot down the bedside runway
for the money shot at the rear.

En plein air

How did the white-haired girl who once
shrieked and cartwheeled across a room,
turn from a buttercream dollop, anxious
to have her way, into such magnificence,
a gentle orchid under a crown of elms?
She turns, like the wheel of years, away,
drawn, *en plein air*, from memory.

Pure snow

(after Miyazawa Kenji)

I have travelled the river of stars
to the last station, the snowy
stop of eternal sleep
where my wild rose
waits for the dew to waken.

From my small, thatched hut
I listen for my lost sister to rouse
in the voices of others I attend—
sick children, tired mothers—
bringing a gift of pure whiteness—
a bowl of snow to eat—
a reason to brighten,
something to delight in.

First and last

Reading the *Man'yōshū*
on a bus to the capital.
Twelve hundred years have passed.
Has anything changed?
I write the saga
of no clan, a bard
of low rank
singing cuckoo songs
for courtiers.

Last supper

On a sill beneath the blue oleanders
his boiled dinner goes untouched.
Why did I make it al dente
when he likes his veggies soft as mush?
My mother is a well of tears.
My wife scolds me for my selfishness.
Ah, the turgor of a firm wedge of cabbage.

Particulars of my trust

Vast as my small demesne
that will and hardship did accrue,
from forgiveness as from strain,
this trust my final due,

my finest gossamer
spun through stingy years.
I leave it all to you—
to you and no other.

Ginkgos in Spring

In the evening darkness
she comes from the distance
bringing a lamp.
         —Bashō

You kneeled on the grass
under the lamp-lit ginkgos.

Now the road is paved.
Green buds are in the treetops.

What happened to that scarf
of golden fans you wore?

How long till you return
lighting my way with your warm glow?

In Yoshiko's apartment

Plato's bust watches me from his pillar.
We listen to Monteverdi.
She is the dark-haired Von Stade
as Penelope, dismissing me
with the crowd of suitors:
Non boglio amar, no no
Ch'amando penero.

I speak one language
but know the meaning
of the scene.

We sit under the *kotatsu*
neat as confectionary
wrapped in crimped
waxed paper, stuck
in a sealed box
we cannot open.

Kamogawa memories

Flowing now with the investment of many,
taking new shape as I turn, what could I say
to you after all these years, our lives so far
from their origins? You were always
of-the-moment, aware of flow and color,
your painter's palette a shield against
my surge, as still-forming headwaters
move to the shape of uncertain boundaries,
unsure at any moment how far to run.

For a time, the old capitol was ours.
We wrote across a table at a coffee shop,
interpreting each other, filling
blank pages like children
inking copybooks in *hiragana*.
But your father called you home
from beyond impenetrable mountains.

I still wonder where you are,
and return to Sakyo-ku in a dream,
carrying your purple bath bucket
so tight its rim leaves a half-moon scar
deep into my breathing, lungs filled
with December's pentathol wind,
the night's vista full of icicle beards
under lamps, snowmounds like the white slab
marking your brother's bones.

I have passed your father's age
and have had to relearn your grammar
to remember our differences.
Past is indistinguishable from present.
The future is not spoken. My pleas
must have sounded ungainly or childish,

the willful and direct a construction
too stark and fragile to be lived in,
best only dreamed or imagined, if then.

I think of the cosmology of circumstance
that keeps us here, entwined as photos stuck
together after decades in a dark drawer.
Your sunlit snapshot nests against my profile
in the old blue passport, blanketed by pages
of bold permits and visas, expired now.

I hear your voice, the tense conditional
offering faint hope of meeting,
and carry, too, the last "Take Care"
you whispered to me like a souvenir.

I am well cared for, though
I cannot break your hold or let go.
Yet what better mistake than to live
with one eye looking back,
the lost dream waxing into clarity.
I have no words to change who I was,
or make time lost seem less worthwhile.
The past makes us no more or less,
a latch that catches but never closes.

Sketch

A sketch she drew—
two strokes of ink
set off by a sunrise
of tangerine pink,

her mischievous eyes
cold stars
far off and elusive—
so she still lives

as beauty is
lit and lost,
cold in its frame
through years of change

as sunset fades
to memory
with long reflection
in its shade.

Of sorrow

I would not go with her
        into the Sonezaki wood
that is the death of love
        but gathered what I could
to feed the feral sorrow
        that slinked within;
When will you be gone
        my unrelieving song?
How long must you cure,
        or will you end with me?
I ask the latest yowl,
        which lessens and lessens still.

Tuning fork

The thwack's vibrato
      shakes the human fork
a bruising echo—
      memory's blood sport—
sating this craving
      to relive old wounds
in renewed vibrations.

A poet's hut

I spend my hours at home,
watching my house fall into disrepair.
The pipes along the risers are exposed.
Mice scamper across my carpet.
Nearing winter, the chimney crumbles.

> *A poet's hut;*
> *renovations are postponed*
> *until the next hurricane.*

Yet I have time to burn.
I compose my *Collection of a Thousand Years,*
an emperor banished by barbarians.

My wealth is what I gather in in my stare,
this harvest a grist of my own making.

> *My purse is empty.*
> *But in the satchel of my cheek*
> *I grind these acorns.*

> *Prolific in death*
> *the old red-faced maple sires*
> *a seedling forest.*

I didn't know Kyoto

I didn't know Kyoto
when I was in Kyoto

walking by the river
holding hands,

visiting the jazz club
north of Shijo.

Was it because
everything was new?

Even the ancient temple,
the old boarding house,

the paths of Mt. Hiei
seemed fresh with dew.

But now I walk with another
in a different village far away

that reminds me of Kitashirakawa,
The same feeling returns

folding laundry, peeling an apple,
binge watching each other.

I am who I want to be
exposed for what I am.

I have found Kyoto,
I have found myself

in a different place,
the old haunts lost and looming

like objects in the mirror,
much closer than they appear.

Memoir

Life is a moment
     until something breaks
that shatters the hardness
     which mending shapes.

Afterword

Writing across cultures—like living with another person—comes with risk. Each cohabitant must be true and give efficacy and voice to the other or risk damaging the relationship. Creating poetry, where language is everything, is enough of a risk not to look for more. Our very lives, our flimsy shelter, are fragile, crumbling from the wear and tear of living.

> A poet's hut;
> renovations must be postponed
> until the next hurricane.

I wrote these poems in a Japanese style known for its immediacy, brevity, unabashed feeling, and ability to evoke loss and the fleetingness of life. The style reflects the intuitive and impulsive aspects of human nature, which can take instantaneous measure of the world and reveal facets of experience and ourselves we tend to hide. The style also illuminates how poems are made—as much from sudden inspiration (an otherworldly gift that lites on tongue) as from an artisan's deft hammering.

From the beginning I recognized it would be fruitless merely to simply copy the style of traditional and modern Japanese writers. The strength of traditional Japanese verse lies in suggestiveness, concision, sudden shifts in perception, and (highly visual) connotation—aspects of a language that is written primarily in Chinese ideograms. The strength of modern Japanese verse lies—in the words of its most exemplary practitioner, Hagiwara Sakutarō—in its purpose: "to complicate the essence of the feeling itself trembling inside the human heart." English verse is propelled not by syllabics and visual cues or the unselfconscious immediacy of emotion but by strong verbs, metrics and pacing, the quirkiness of voice, and rhyme (which, for me, can be used to fortify a feeling).

I also recognized the trap of appropriating another culture and dealt with that directly. One of the poems is a response to Takamura Kōtarō's ridicule of Western writers who drape themselves in "Japon" (the mystery of the East) as if it were an article of their own clothing.

The title of this collection comes from a haiku by Bashō.

> *Even in Kyoto*
> *hearing the cry of the cuckoo*
> *I long for Kyoto.*

For me it captures the essence of haiku, the skillful, off-hand, freeze frame of a sudden awareness that is hard to grasp, and, in the moment of clarity, leaves the previous state of consciousness behind. Kyoto is still there but lost. From a Buddhist perspective, it is not possible to know place and time, for even the ground we walk on is an illusion. In a Lafcadio Hearn twice-told Buddhist tale, a man reaches the summit of a mountain that crumbles beneath him. The mountain, the man realizes, comprises the shards of skulls that hold all his forgotten dreams.

Many of these small poems pinpoint a moment of sudden awareness or focus on a delusion or obsession, another common feature of Japanese literature that is the stock and trade of writers like Tanizaki or Takuboku, for whom perversity is a generous talent.

Mostly, they pay homage to the purity with which Japanese writers express complex emotion. Though my own poems originate sometimes more in memory than in the moment, no matter the language of creation or approximation, or differences of belief or the gulf across years, poetry has one mission: to speak to and through the heart.

Sheppard Ranbom
Washington, DC
November 2021

Sources and Suggested Reading

For readers interested in learning more about Japanese poetry and the influences in this book, I recommend the following:

Matsuo Bashō, *The Narrow Road to the Deep North and Other Travel Sketches*, translated by Nobuyiki Yuasa, Penguin Classics, 1967

Sakutaro Hagiwara, *Cat Town*, translated by Hiroaki Sato, New York Review Books, 2014

Robert Haas, editor, *The Essential Haiku: Versions of Basho, Buson and Issa*, Harper Collins, 1995

Donald Keene, *Dawn to the West, Japanese Literature of the Modern Era* (Poetry, Drama, Criticism), Holt, Rinehart and Winston, 1984

Donald Keene, *Japanese Literature: An Introduction for Western Readers*, Grove Press, 1955

Donald Keene, *Landscapes and Portraits: Appreciations of Japanese Culture*, Kodansha International, Ltd., 1971

Donald Keene, *The First Modern Japanese: The Life of Ishikawa Takaboku*, Columbia University Press, 2016

Donald Keene, *World Within Walls, Japanese Literature of the Pre-Modern Era 1600-1867*, Holt, Rinehart and Winston, 1972

J. Thomas Rimer and Van C. Gessel, editors, *The Columbia Anthology of Modern Japanese Literature, Volume I: From Restoration to Occupation, 1868-1945,* Columbia University Press, 2005

Hiroaki Sato and Burton Watson, translators and editors, *From the Country of Eight Islands: An Anthology of Japanese Poetry*, Doubleday and Company, 1981

Ishikwa Takuboku, *Romaji Diary and Sad Toys* translated and edited by Sanford Goldstein and Seishi Shinoda, Charles E. Tuttle, 2000

Junichiro Tanizaki, *Diary of a Mad Old Man*, translated by Howard Hibbett, Alfred A. Knopf, 1965

Junichiro Tanizaki, *Naomi*, translated by Anthony Chambers, Northpoint Press, 1990

Junichiro Tanizaki, *Seven Japanese Tales*, translated by Howard Hibbett, Alfred A. Knopf, 1963

Junichiro Tanizaki, *Some Prefer Nettles*, translated by Edward G. Seidensticker, Berkeley Publishing, 1960

Junichiro Tanizaki, *The Key*, translated by Howard Hibbett, Alfred A. Knopf, 1960

Junichirio Tanizaki, *The Makioka Sisters*, translated by Edward G. Seidensticker, Vintage International, 1985

Junichiro Tanizaki, *The Secret History of the Lord of Musahi* and *Arrowroot*, translated by Anthony Chambers, Vintage International, 2003

Akiko Yosano, *Tangled Hair*, translated by Sanford Goldstein and Seishi Shinoda, Charles E. Tuttle, 1993

Sheppard Ranbom is the author of two books of poetry: *King Philip's War*, a book-length poem that tells the story of the genocide of the New England Algonquians, and *I Didn't Know Kyoto*, a series of poems written in a Japanese style that explores the author's romance with Japan and—based on an ill-fated love affair—the beauty that can be found in suffering.

In addition, he has recently completed a play—*The Love Suicides at Takayama*—and two additional poetry books—a novella in verse and a collection of poems written over the past 20 years—that will be forthcoming.

He is the co-founder, with his wife, Mary-Mack Callahan, of CommunicationWorks, LLC a national public-affairs firm focused on education, higher education, workforce, and civil rights issues based in Washington, DC that he has led for nearly 30 years.

He began his career as an assistant to the book review editor at the national publication, Books & Arts, and then as a journalist focusing on schools and higher education.

Through his long career in journalism and public affairs, he wrote an award-winning book-length series of articles, *Schooling in Japan: The Paradox in the Pattern for Education Week*, and countless reports and whitepapers for his clients on scores of issues in K-12 and higher education. He continues to ghostwrite articles for his clients that appear in national and regional newspapers, magazines, and trade publications. He also has written extensively about theatre and the fine arts, including an introduction to the paintings of American landscape artists Michele Martin Taylor and Andrei Kushnir.

To read his thoughts about poetry, literature, authors, and life— and occasional works in progress—visit his blog, https://www.sheppardranbom.com/blog